The Pick-A-

By Stephen J. Falvo

Illustrated by Vincente Rangel

The Pick-A-Roo

ISBN: 978-1484074695

Copyright © 2013 Stephen J. Falvo

Illustrations copyright © 2013 Vincente Rangel

First Printing: April 2013

Produced by Social Incites, LLC
www.socialincites.com

Holland, Michigan

To Noah, our little "Bug-A-Boo."

"The Pick-A-Roo" is a true story
based on actual events that happened to my younger
brother during his Little League baseball days.
Thanks, Spencer, for inspiring this story, and for your
willingness to let me to share it with others.

Thank you also to my mom, Lauretta Burrows,
and to my wife, Laurel,
both of whom encouraged me and helped me
to develop this story into a book.

Whenever

I'm asked

to share a

story,

or fable,

or two,

I oft' tell the tale of *The Pick-A-Roo.*

Now, "Pick" was the name that they gave him for short,

And quite often did it make them **contort!**

It all began in games

on the baseball field...

As he threw,

Or he caught,

Or his bat,

he did wield.

He did play the game of baseball quite well,

But upon that point,

no one would dwell.

The trouble would usually start

before windup, or after a pitch,

When he **tugged** at the seat of his pants with an **itch**.

Whether in dugout,

on field,

or at plate,

His uncouth habit

simply wouldn't abate!

Each time he tugged at his little caboose,

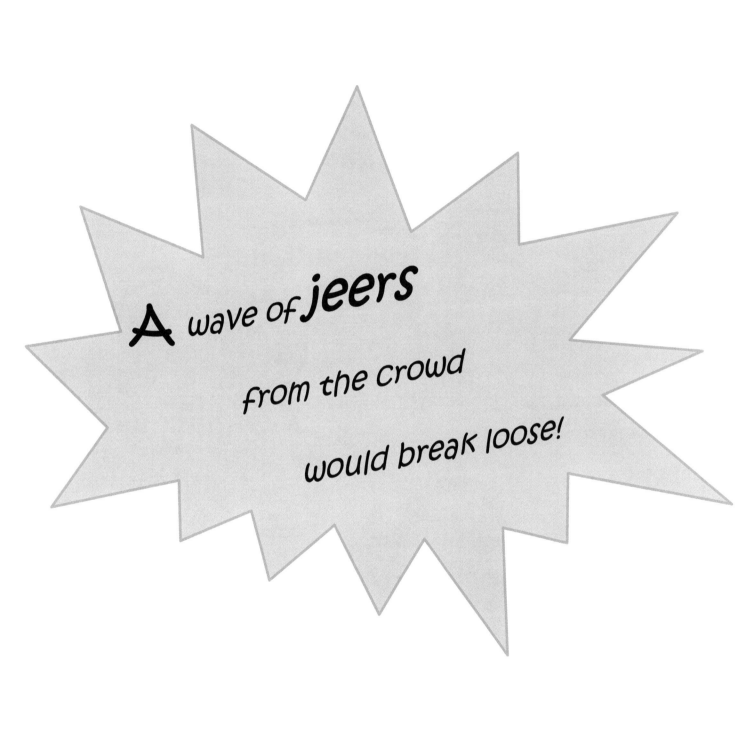

They would

shout,

as the umpire

cried,

"Strike three!"

His parents said,

"You could have picked your **nose** or your **teeth**.
You could have even picked the **dirt** from your **cleats!**"

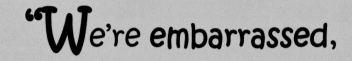

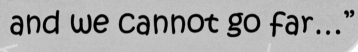

"**W**ithout hearing talk of our son,
and a **hardy, har har!**"

Now, some people wondered, and others did ask,

He told her they fit,

and that there wasn't a problem,

But...

he continued to **pick** and **tug** at his bottom.

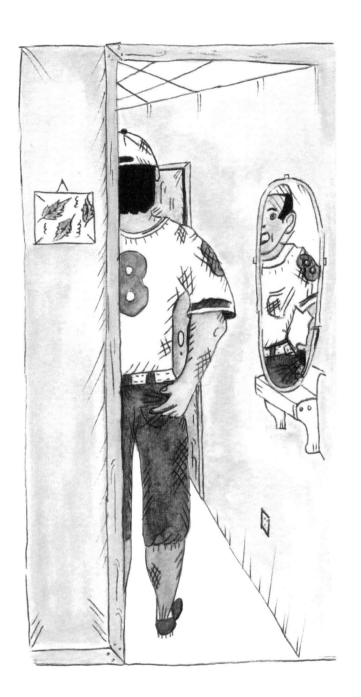

Pick...

Pick...

Pick-a-Roo....

It was much like a sneeze without the

"A-choo!"

One day, after making a special trip

to the store,

The name,

"Pick-A-Roo,"

he would hear no more.

His itching, it seems,

had been caused by his **briefs!**

From this short story,

there must be a reason,

To share it again,

in just the right season.

For when it is hot,

or on ground there lies dew,

And all
of your
clothes try
to stick upon
you...

Or the name

"Pick-A-Roo"

you may too,

have to lug!

About the Author:

Stephen Falvo is the author of a variety of books. "The Pick-A-Roo" is his first children's book and is based on his brother's Little League baseball days. Mr. Falvo loves to play basketball, ride bikes, go boating, and to write and share stories. He resides in Michigan with his wife Laurel and their four children. He and his wife operate Social Incites, LLC, a social coaching business that helps individuals and families improve their ability to succeed in their personal and professional lives through better social understanding.

Connect with "Steve Falvo" on Facebook to ask questions, share encouragement, and follow updates on new resources!

About the Illustrator:

Vincente Rangel is a talented illustrator who has had his work featured in several books. From his beginnings in south Texas to his current residence in Michigan, Mr. Rangel's abilities are expressed with versatility and a flair for helping bring a story to life. He lives in Michigan with his wife and four sons.

Made in the USA
Charleston, SC
21 November 2013